THE THINGS CHEMISTS USE IN CHEMICAL LABS

6TH GRADE CHEMISTRY
CHILDREN'S CHEMISTRY BOOKS

Speedy Publishing LLC
40 E. Main St. #1156
Newark, DE 19711
www.speedypublishing.com

Chemists study how elements and compounds react with each other, how they change when heated or cooled, and above all what we can do with the results of the changes. Step into a chemistry lab and see what's there!

Laboratory

WORKING IN A LAB

You can do some simple experiments with very little equipment, right in your own kitchen. However, chemists usually work in a special room or building that has all the equipment they are likely to need: the chemistry laboratory. Having everything in one place makes it easy to work well without delays while you try to find some piece of equipment.

It also means you have a safe, clean place to keep your equipment, an experiment in progress, and the notes you are taking about it. Having a space with doors and windows that can close keeps people, animals, and just plain dust from messing up your experiments!

Here are some of the things you'll find in a well-equipped chemistry lab:

SAFETY EQUIPMENT

The first rule in any laboratory is to be safe. You don't want to hurt yourself, the people in the lab with you, or the people who will use the lab in the future. It's important to take care of yourself and keep the equipment in good repair.

PROTOCOLS

Most labs have checklists for the standard things you need to do. All these little steps may seem like a waste of time, but in a good checklist every step is there for a reason. One of the biggest reasons is to keep you safe! If you are going to work with chemicals, open flames, and other potentially-dangerous factors, find out the lab protocols before you start.

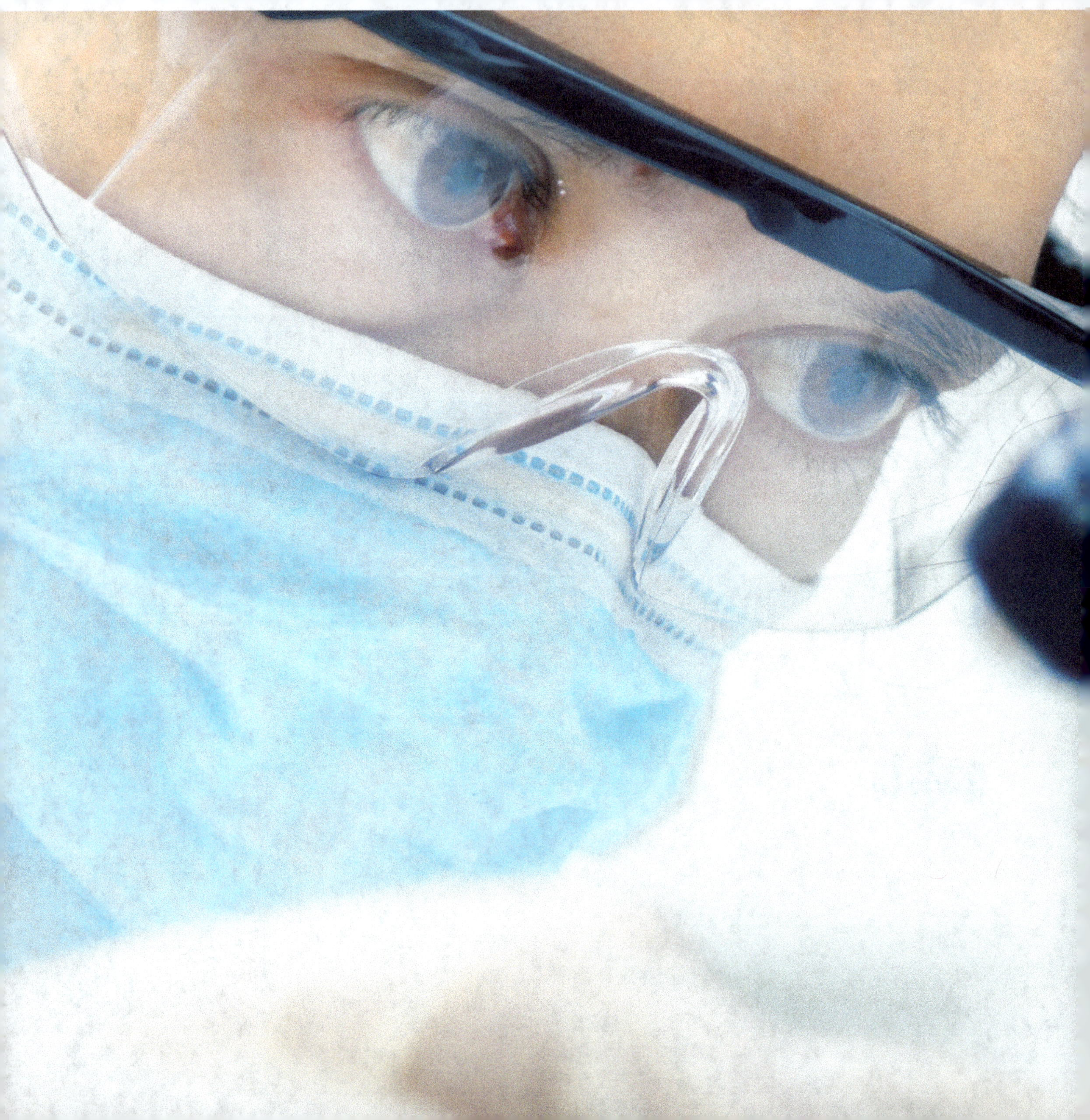

SAFETY GOGGLES

Safety goggles protect your eyes from splashes, tiny particles of chemicals floating in the air, and even shards of glass if something should fall and break. Good safety goggles fit over your regular glasses, if you wear them, and after a few minutes you will hardly notice they are there. But they help keep you safe.

Scientists eyes protected with safety goggles as he conducts certain activities in laboratory.

PROTECTIVE GLOVES

Chemists wear gloves to protect themselves from things spilling onto their hands and possibly hurting them. It also protects them from adding dirt or sweat from their fingers to whatever they are working on.

Chemist hands protected with rubber gloves.

LAB COAT

Chemists wear a lab coat or a protective apron to protect against spills. It also helps keep the fibers from their own clothing out of the material of their experiment!

COMMON SENSE!

Chemists with beards or long hair wear hair nets or hats to keep their hair from contaminating the experiment. All chemists wear closed shoes, not sandals, and avoid high heels: you want to keep your feet safe from things that fall or drip off a surface.

Lab chemist working with microscope and tubes.

Glass beaker with flask in background.

BEAKERS AND FLASKS

BEAKERS

Chemists use beakers for mixing, stirring, and heating chemicals. Beakers often have a spout at one point on the rim to make it easier to pour out the contents. They come in many different sizes.

1000
APPROX
800
600
400

ERLENMEYER FLASK

The Erlenmeyer Flask has a narrow neck and a much wider base. This lets you mix and even swirl the contents of the flask with less risk of spilling. You can also put a rubber or glass stopper in the mouth of the neck to protect the contents. But never heat the flask while a stopper is in place: it could explode!

A studio photo of a Erlenmeyer Flask.

FLORENCE FLASK

A Florence Flask, or Boiling Flask, has a long neck and a round bottom. It can be heated or capped with a stopper--but not both at the same time!

Boiling chemical liquid in florence flask.

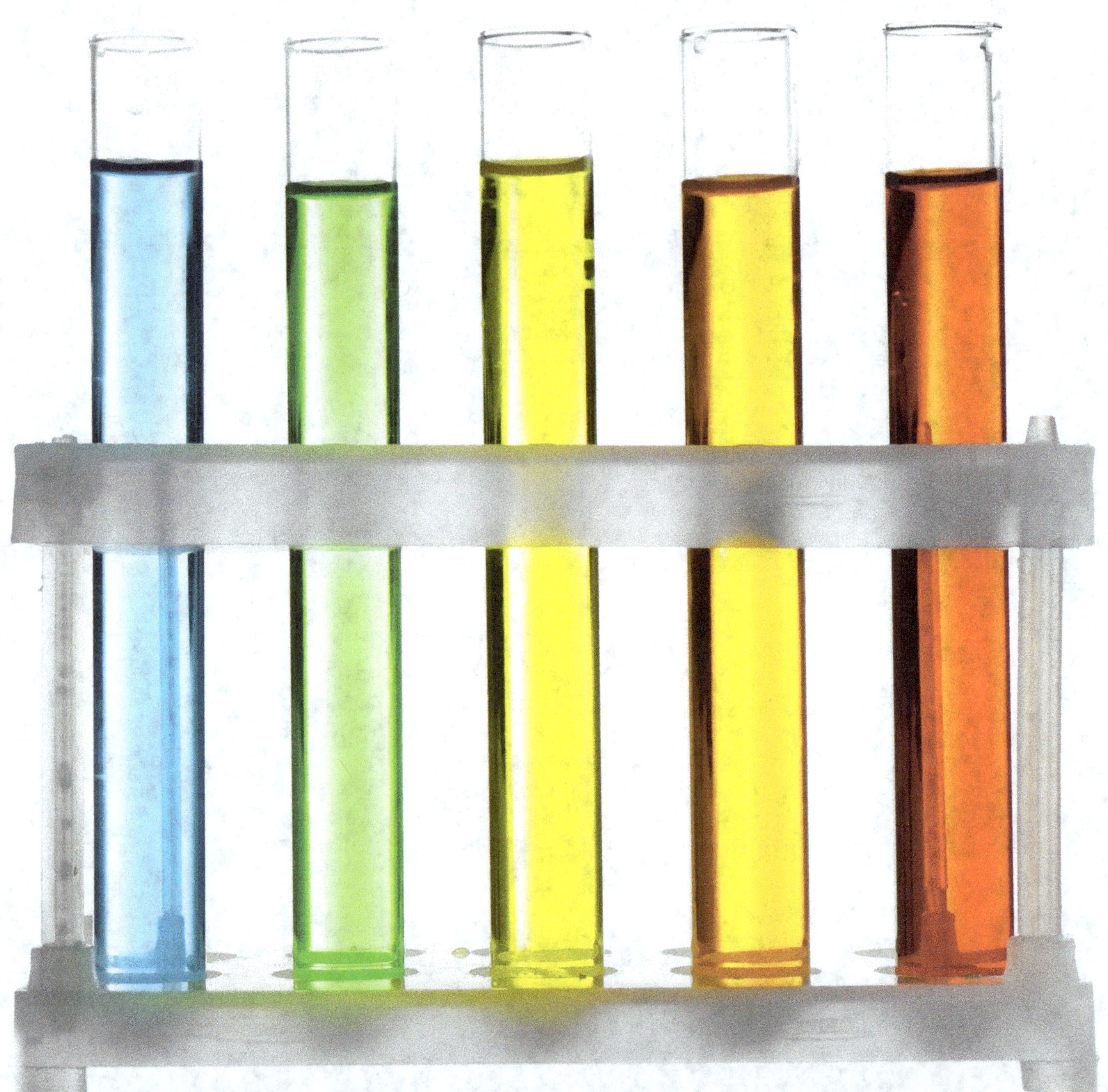

TEST TUBES

A Test Tube has an open end and a rounded, closed end. Test Tubes hold small samples, especially when the chemist is comparing samples from several different mixtures or sources. When there are more than a few test tubes, the scientist puts them in a rack, and keeps records of what is in which Test Tube.

Test tubes with colorful samples on stand.

Bunsen flame and a glass stand

CONTROLLED HEAT

When working with chemicals and heat, you need a heat source and a way of measuring the temperature of whatever you are heating.

BUNSEN BURNER

Bunsen burners are standard lab tools. They are attached to a source of flammable gas, and have a knob so you can adjust how much gas is flowing. You open the flow a little bit and light the burner with a "striker", and then adjust the gas flow and air flow to get the flame you want.

Bunsen burners are as useful, and as dangerous, as any other open flame. Be very careful when working with them!

Microbiological inoculation loop heated by a bunsen burner.

THERMOMETER

There are many kinds of lab thermometers to measure the temperature of liquids. They are often made of glass, or of a combination of metals making a "thermocouple".

Thermometer in glass flask.

Laboratory glassware with laboratory microscope.
250ml
±5%
250ml
200
150
100

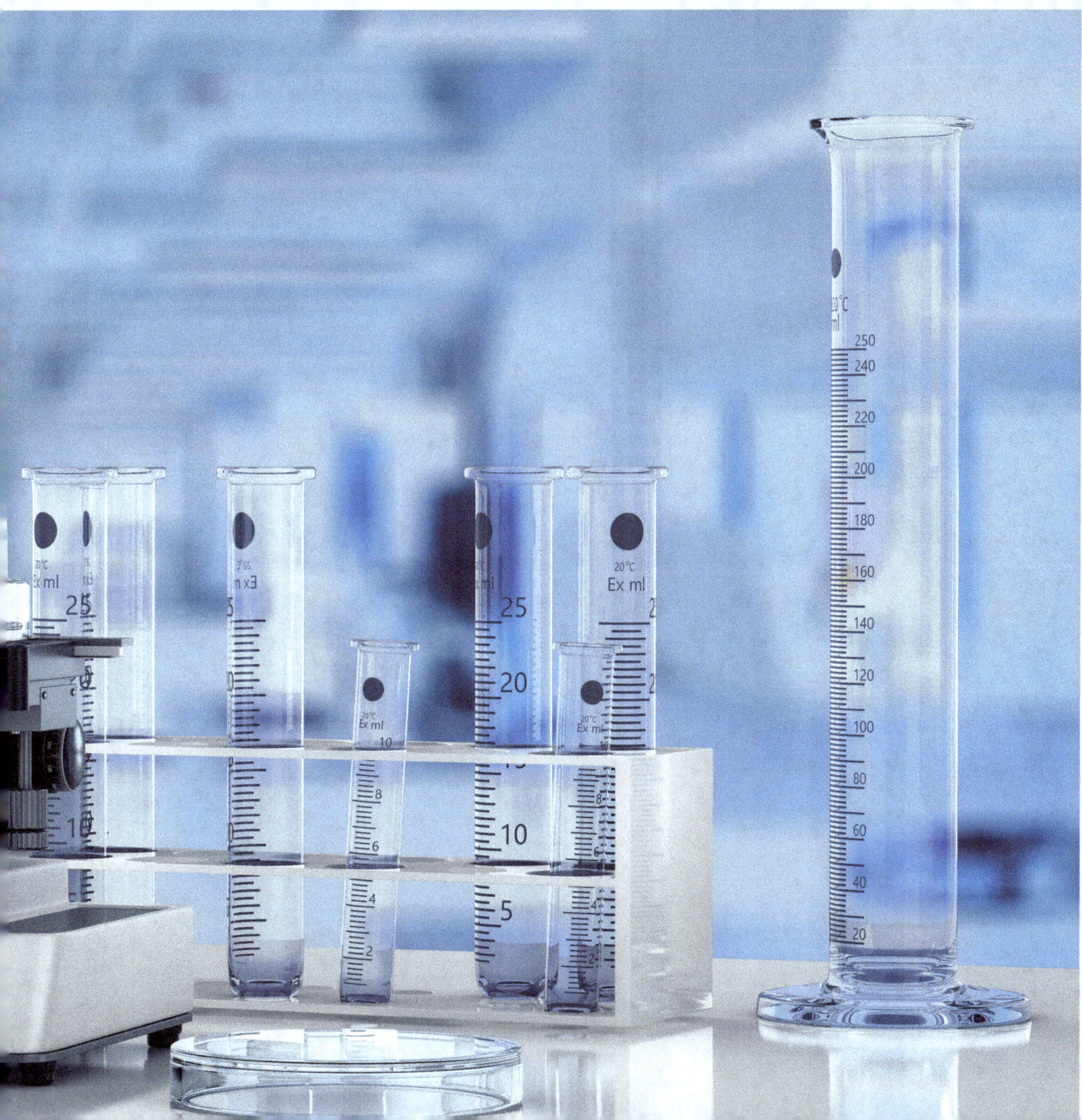

GETTING THE RIGHT AMOUNT

For your experiment, or to make your compound, you need the right amount of each chemical. To understand what happened in your experiment, you also need to know how much of each chemical you started with.

GRADUATED CYLINDER

To measure the volume of a liquid, scientists use graduated cylinders. There are markings up the side of the cylinder so you can see how much it contains.

VOLUMETRIC FLASK

A volumetric flask is round, with a flat bottom and a long neck. Chemists use it for exact measurements of the volume of a liquid. Volumetric flasks come in different standard sizes, so you just fill up the one you want to the indicator line--like using measuring spoons in your kitchen.

Graduated Cylinder

Laboratory pipette and glass test tubes.

DROPPER

A Dropper is a small glass tube with a narrow opening at one end and a rubber bulb at the other. When you squeeze the bulb you push air out of the tube; then insert the other end in a liquid and relax the bulb to draw some of the liquid into the Dropper. Then you can squeeze the bulb again to put the liquid you gathered where you want it.

PIPETTE

Pipettes are another type of tool for getting the exact amount of liquid that you want and moving it to another container.

BURET

Buret is a glass tube with a controlled opening at the bottom, and is usually attached to a ring stand with a clamp. You can open the control at the bottom to let out more or less of the liquid in the buret.

BALANCE

Balance helps you weigh chemicals you are going to use. You put the container with the chemical on one side of the balance, and add weights to the other side until the balance is level.

Buret filled with yellow liquid in laboratory.

Funnel, beaker and flasks in laboratory.

OTHER TOOLS

There are many other tools that can help you do your experiments. Here are some:

WATCH GLASS

A watch glass is like a small, shallow glass plate. It can hold a small amount of a liquid or solid. People also use them as temporary lids for beakers.

CRUCIBLE

A Crucible is a small container made of clay. You can use a crucible for heating substances to very high temperatures.

FUNNEL

Funnels have a wide end you pour things into and a narrow end the stuff comes out through. They help you not make a mess when you are adding chemicals to a container!

RING STAND, RINGS AND CLAMPS

You can use Clamps or Rings to attach containers to a Ring Stand, either because the container has a round bottom or because you want to put the container over a Bunsen burner to heat it.

Make sure everything is clamped securely, and be careful when clamping glass containers to avoid cracking or breaking them. You also have to be sure the ring stand is balanced, and will not just fall over when you let go of it.

Retort stand clamp holding a conical glass flask.

TONGS AND FORCEPS

You use tongs and forceps to take hold of things you should not touch with your hand. This is to prevent you contaminating the experiment with material from your hand or glove, and also to protect your hands from the chemicals and from heat.

Forceps are smaller holders, like tweezers. You can use them to take hold of small parts of solid chemicals and move the amount you want to another container.

Scientist using the forceps in plant tissue culture laboratory.

SPATULAS AND SCOOPULAS

Scoopulas and spatulas are for getting small amounts of solid chemicals. You scoop up some of the chemical and put it in a container on one side of a balance, and keep adding more scoops until you have the amount of the chemical that you need.

spatulas and scoopulas

KEEPING RECORDS

It is really important to keep track of what you are doing in the lab! Chemists use paper or computer tools to record what they did and what they discovered.

WORKSHEETS AND NOTEBOOKS

Scientists use worksheets to write down notes as they prepare for and conduct an experiment, and notebooks to keep long-term records. These records can be on sheets of paper or on a computer.

LAB REPORT

A lab report is a formal summary of what you did, what you used to do it, and what you found. Other scientists can use your report to double-check your work.

SCIENCE IS AMAZING!

The world is full of wonders for you to discover. Read other Baby Professor books like Peeling the Earth like an Onion to learn more!

Visit

BABY PROFESSOR
EDUCATION KIDS

www.BabyProfessorBooks.com
to download Free Baby Professor eBooks
and view our catalog of new and exciting
Children's Books